GRADE 3 SOCIAL SCIENCE

Fun-filled Activities

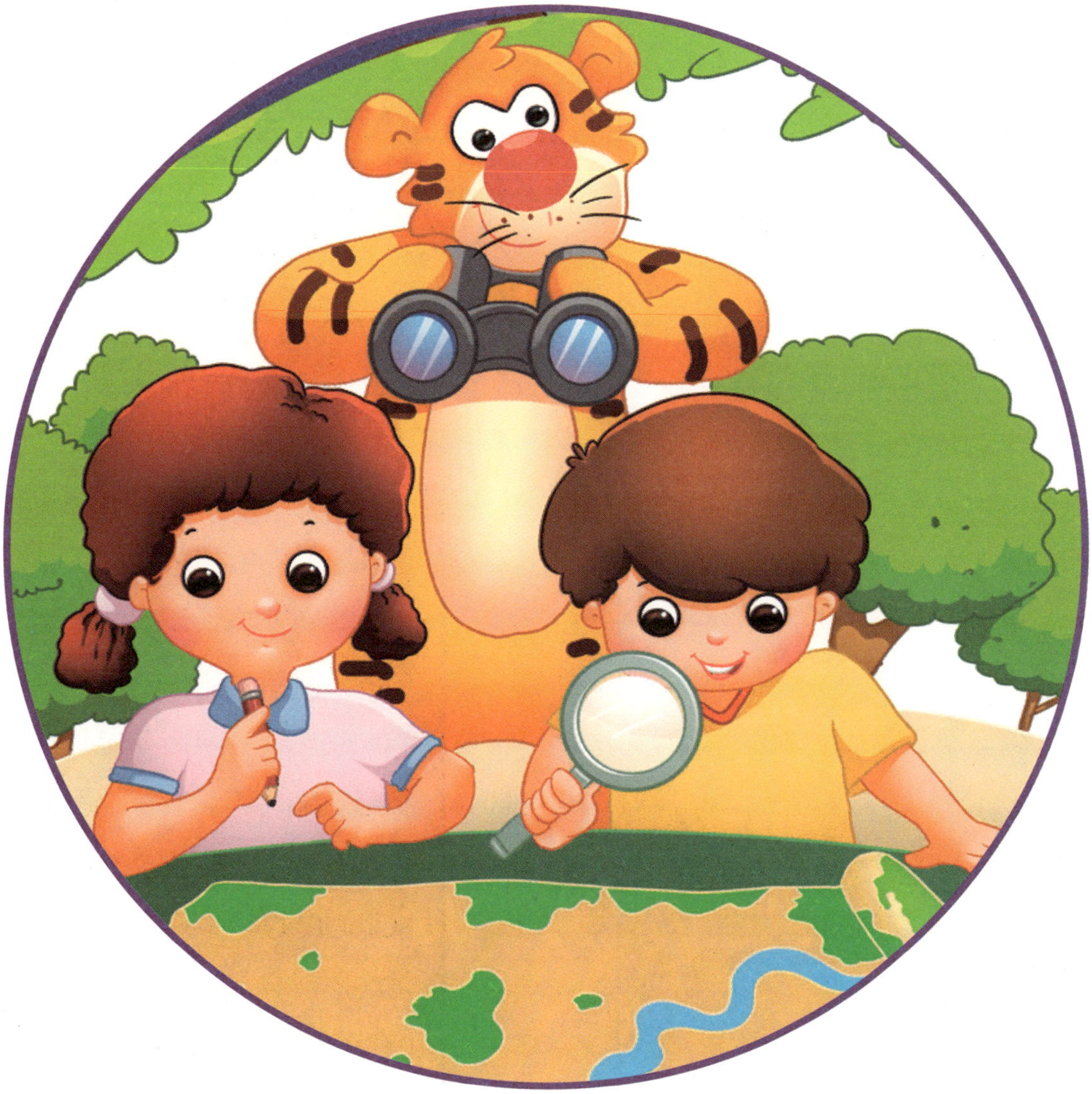

Om KIDZ
An imprint of Om Books International

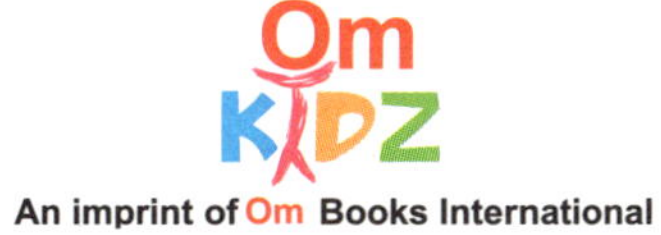

Communities

Robbie has sent postcards to his friends. Use the words in the word bank to fill in the blanks in each postcard.

Hi everyone,

I am enjoying the city. It is an ________ community. I have ridden in ________ and on ________. I have been to the ________ and seen lots of ________. I love it here!

Hi friends,

I am just outside the city in a ________ community. I am staying at my aunt's ________. She has a ________ and a vegetable ________ in her ________. I am having a nice time here.

Hi Kim,

I am staying on a ________ that grows ________. The homes are far apart in the ________ community. I got to ride a ________ and even ________. See you soon!

Your Community

Tick the most appropriate descriptions about your community.

In my community I see:

people	few	☐	several	☐	many	☐
animals	yes	☐	no	☐		
dwellings	houses	☐	apartments	☐	trailers	☐
businesses	restaurant	☐	gas station	☐	bank	☐
	grocers	☐	others ___________			
school	yes	☐	no	☐		
post office	yes	☐	no	☐		
playground	yes	☐	no	☐		
park	yes	☐	no	☐		
transportation	cars	☐	buses	☐	trains	☐
	subways	☐	others ___________			
street lights	few	☐	several	☐	many	☐

Interdependence of Individuals

All individuals in a community are dependent on each other.

Observe the picture carefully and answer the questions.

1. How many people are acting as helping hands in the picture? Name them.

   ____

2. How does the police officer help the fire fighters?

   ____

3. Why is it necessary to have emergency medical services in a community?

   ____

4. Name any five community helpers other than those in the picture and write their roles.

   ____

Try it! Make a diorama of your community and display it in the class. Write the name of your community and important places on the diorama.

Community Laws

Every community has certain laws and rules. Laws are important to keep a community in order.

Read the statements below. Tick any five rules you think are most important.

- [ ] Obey traffic lights.
- [ ] Wear seat belts.
- [ ] No littering.
- [ ] Do not take things that belong to someone else.
- [ ] Keep pets on a leash.
- [ ] Wear a helmet when you ride a bike.
- [ ] Do not damage public property.

Write why you chose each one of them.

1. ______________________________

2. ______________________________

3. ______________________________

4. ______________________________

5. ______________________________

My Rules

Fill in word or phrase that best completes the sentence. Colour the box with the given colour code.

home rule= yellow
school rule = red
community rule = blue

- [ ] 1. Be responsible for ________________ (learning how to cook, your pets)
- [ ] 2. ______________ in the haste. (Don't run, Go to school)
- [ ] 3. ______________ litter. (Don't, Do)
- [ ] 4. Do your ____________ (chores, mail)
- [ ] 5. Finish your __________ (drawing, homework)
- [ ] 6. Share your toys ________________ (with your brothers and sisters, on Mondays)
- [ ] 7. Wear a __________ (hat, bike helmet)
- [ ] 8. ______________ to your teacher. (Give a plant, Listen)
- [ ] 9. Obey _____________ (traffic rules, the forest)
- [ ] 10. _______________ the people in your family. (Follow, Respect)

Rights and Responsibilities

We all have certain rights and responsibilities in our community.

For instance, we have a right to enjoy the safe and happy place to live. It is our responsibility to keep our community safe and happy.

Read each sentence and write it under the correct heading.

My Community Rights	My Community Responsibilities

I put litter in the dustbin.	I reuse as many things as I can.
I follow road signs.	I play at a neighbourhood park.
I can count on others if I need help.	I check out books from the library.
I help others in need.	I keep my pets from roaming in the community.
My community is a safe place.	The people of my community care for each other.

Making Good Choices

Samuel wants to make good choices. Write to tell what he should do. Explain your answers.

Samuel finds a dollar in the school playground, What should he do?

____

____

____

____

Samuel's teacher is giving instructions. His classmate is whispering to him. What should he do?

____

____

____

____

The class is voting for class president. Samuel doesn't know who to vote for. What should he do?

____

____

____

____

Samuel doesn't know the answers for a few questions in his class test. He wants to ask his classmate for help. What should he do?

____

____

____

____

Samuel wants to go for a match but has his assignment pending. What should he do?

____

____

____

____

Community Workers

Community workers provide different goods and services to the people living in the community. Find about any four workers in your community and fill in the boxes below,

Community worker ______________ Provides ______________ Tools or equipment ______________ Job description ______________________________ ______________________________	Community worker ______________ Provides ______________ Tools or equipment ______________ Job description ______________________________ ______________________________
Community worker ______________ Provides ______________ Tools or equipment ______________ Job description ______________________________ ______________________________	Community worker ______________ Provides ______________ Tools or equipment ______________ Job description ______________________________ ______________________________

Cardinal Points

There are four main directions that help us know our way around the world in which we live. These directions are north, south, east and west. These directions are referred to as cardinal points.

Cardinal points are shown on maps by the use of a compass rose.

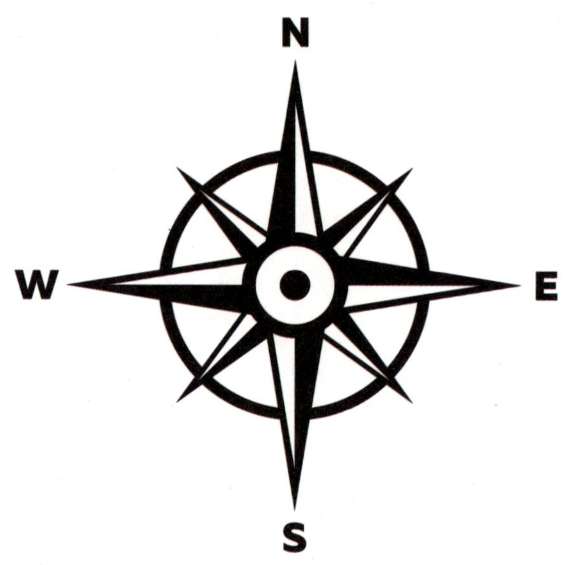

Fill in the cardinal points that are missing.

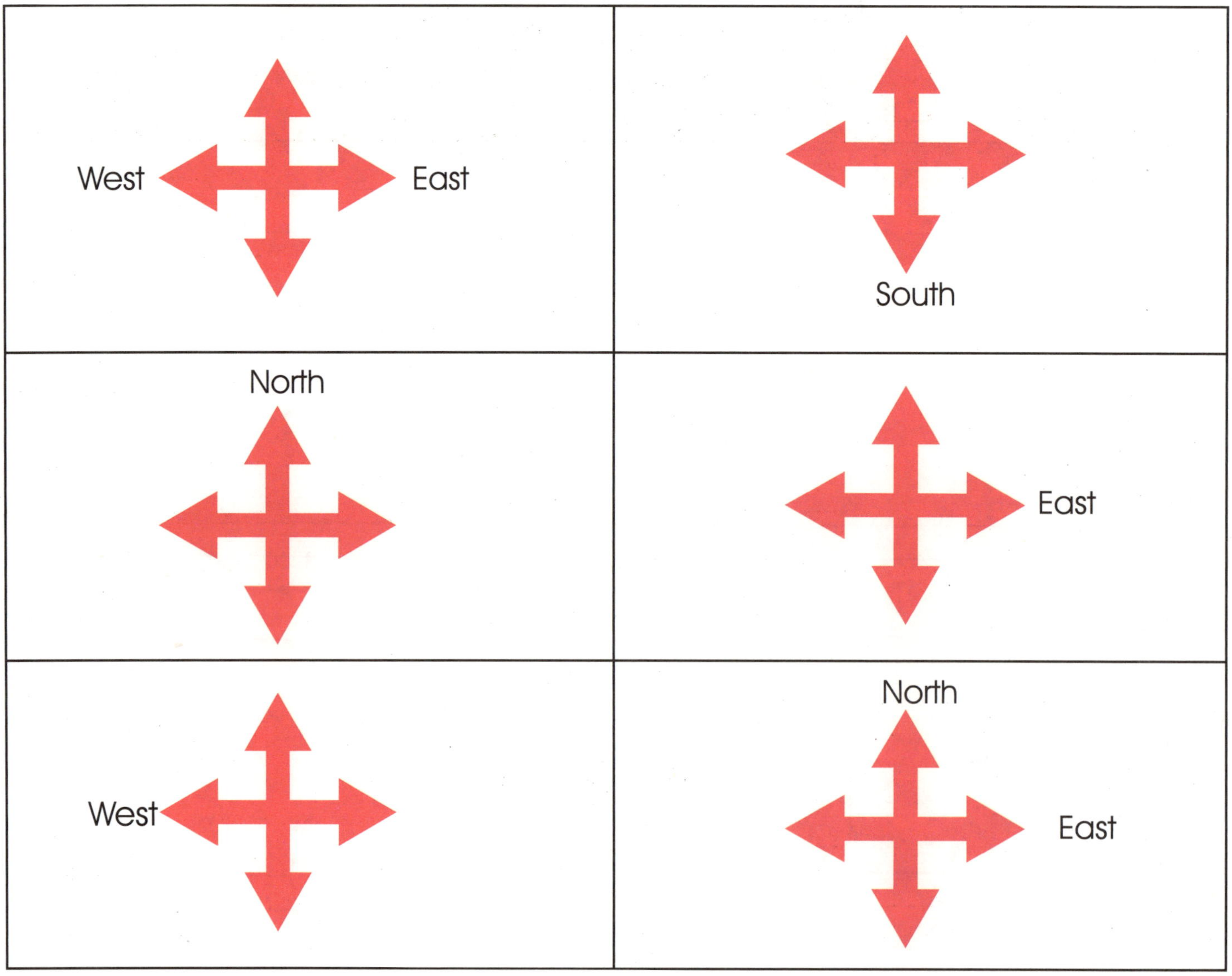

West, East	South
North	East
West	North, East

Intermediate Points

You are now familiar with the four cardinal points. There are times when we can't use just north, south, east and west to give directions. We need to show points that come in between the four primary directions. Intermediate points give a mapmaker such a tool. The intermediate directions are:

NE- northeast
SE- southeast
SW- southwest
NW- northwest

Write the locations of the numbers in the boxes using the cardinal and intermediate directions.

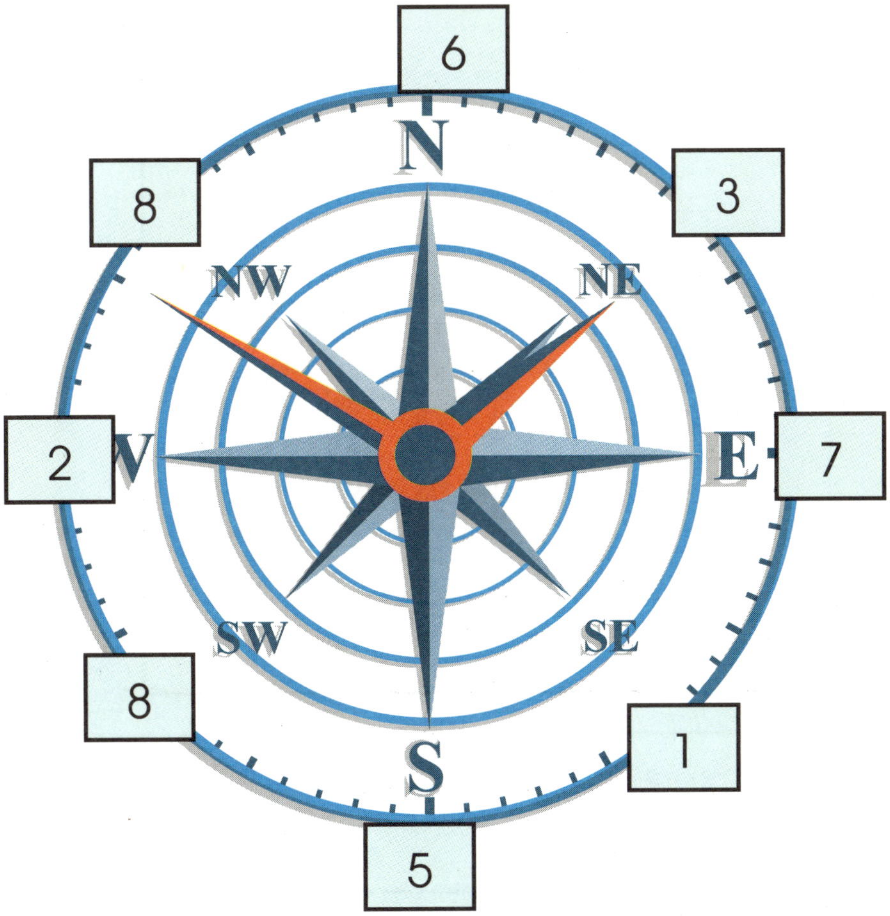

1. ____________________
2. ____________________
3. ____________________
4. ____________________
5. ____________________
6. ____________________
7. ____________________
8. ____________________

Map Grid

Some maps have grids on them.
A grid is a pattern of lines that cross to form squares. Each square on a grid has a letter and a number. A grid makes it easier to locate places on a map.

How to study a grid?

Look at the letter A on the top of the grid.

Then locate the number 1 at the left side of the grid.

We name the first square in the top row as A1.

The second square is A2 and so on.

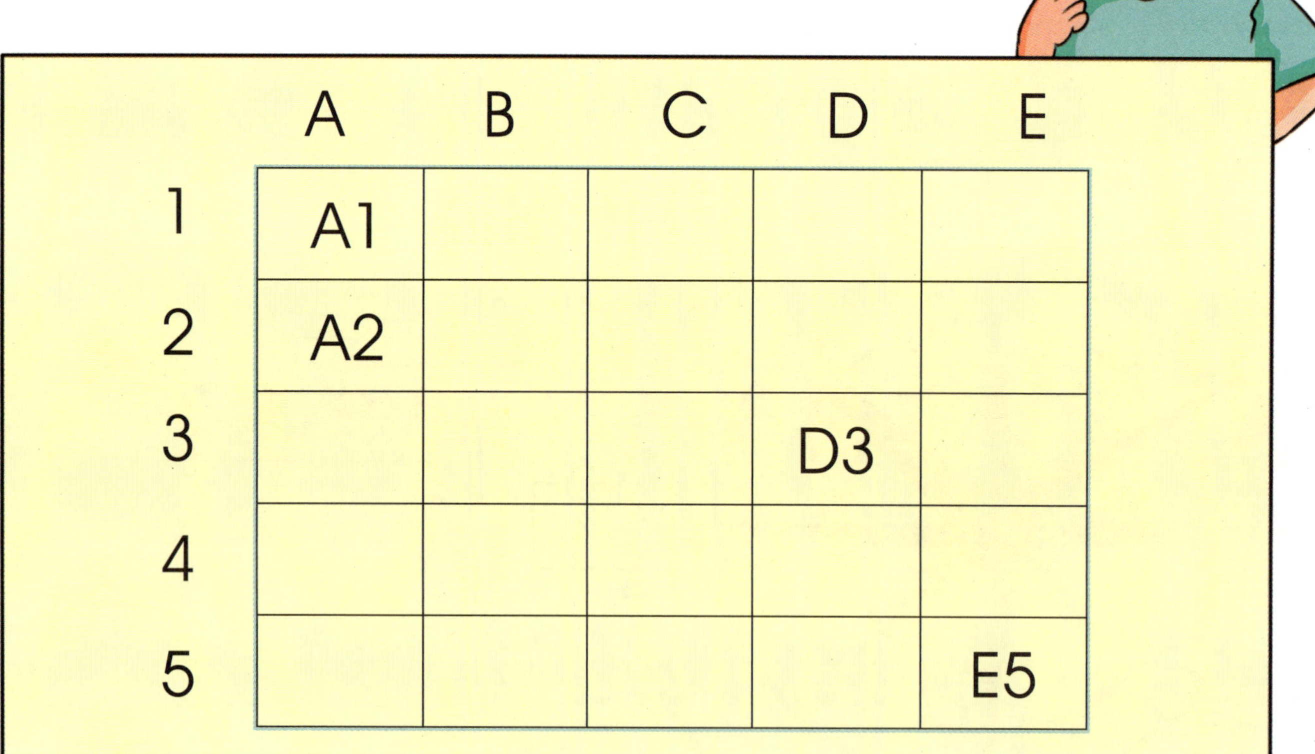

Try it! Make a grid showing the position of three objects in your classroom. Write directions to move from one object to another.

Using Map Grids

Jacob is at the Alfred Nature's Centre. Look at the symbols below and draw them on the grid to complete it.

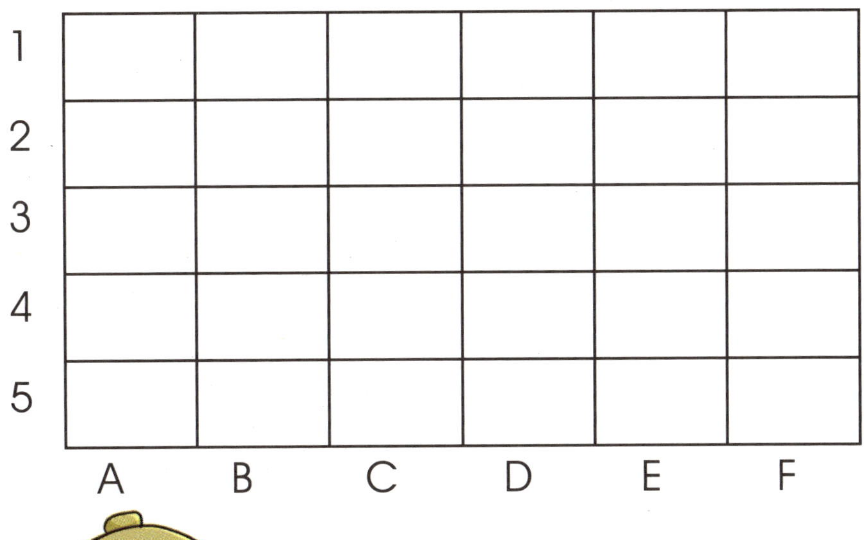

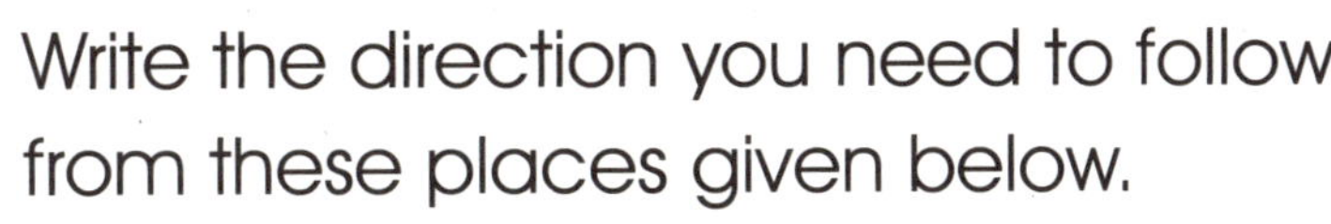

Write the direction you need to follow from these places given below.

1. From flower display to insect display
2. From help desk to snacks counter
3. From fish display to wildlife display
4. From tree display to maps

      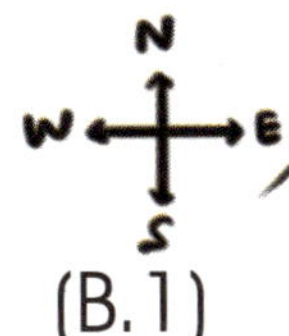

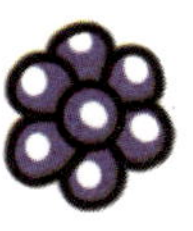  

(E.5) (C.3) (A.1) (E.3) (A.4) (B.1) (C.5) (E.1)

Using Cardinal Directions

Help Paul find the objects on the map. Follow the clues and draw the object you land on in the box.

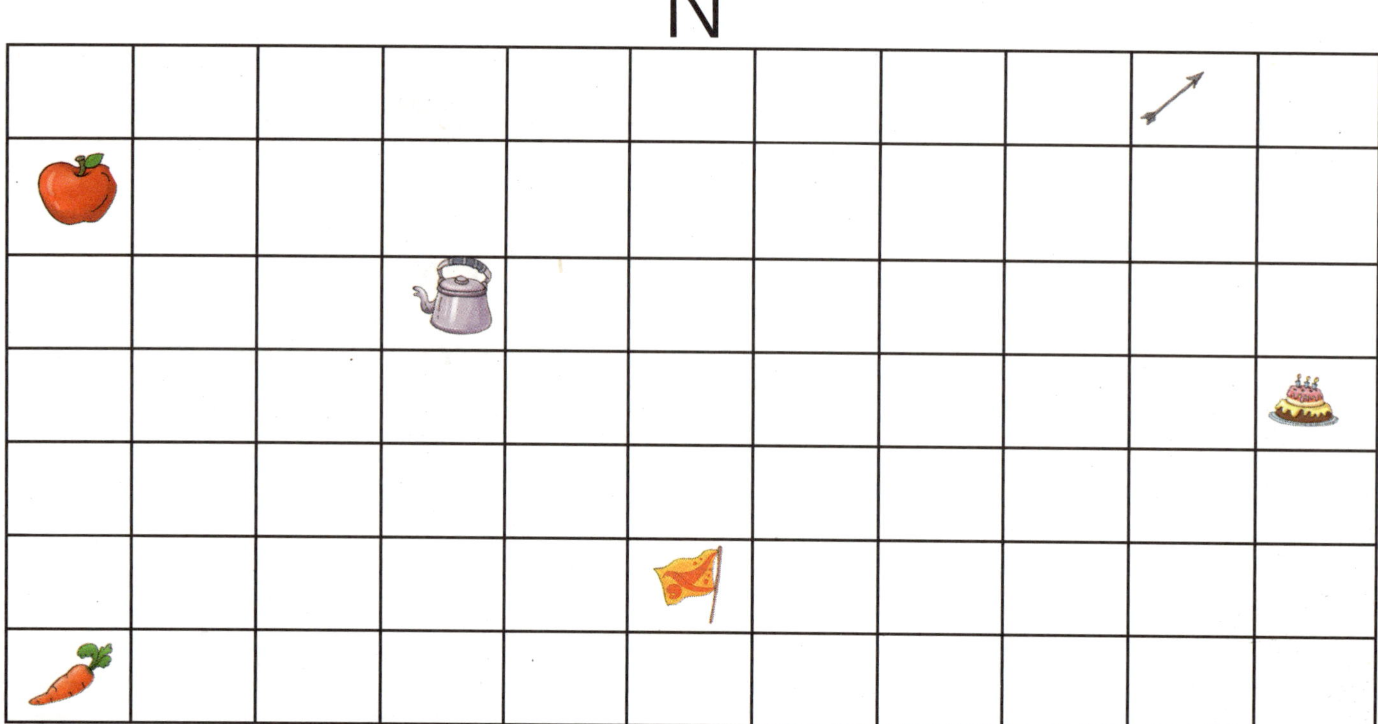

Start at the apple. Go east 3 boxes. Then go south 1 box. Draw a picture of the object you landed on.	Start at the flag. Go north 2 boxes. Then go east 5 boxes. Draw a picture of the object you landed on.
Start at the carrot. Go east 5 boxes. Then go north 1 box. Draw a picture of the object you landed on.	Start at the flag. Go west 5 boxes. Then go south 1 box. Draw a picture of the object you landed on.
Start at the arrow. Go east 1 box. Then go south 3 boxes. Draw a picture of the object you landed on.	Start at the carrot. Go north 5 boxes. Draw a picture of the object you landed on.

Map Skills

Read the statements below and draw the picture of the characters in the map .

1. The old woman's house is on the West Gits Road.
2. The cow is in the barnyard.
3. The horse is in the North Grassland.
4. The farmer is in the East Field.
5. The mower is at the South Gate.
6. The gingerbread boy is near the tree west of barnyard.
7. The fox is to the west of the Duck Pond.

Map Skills

Study the map and the key.

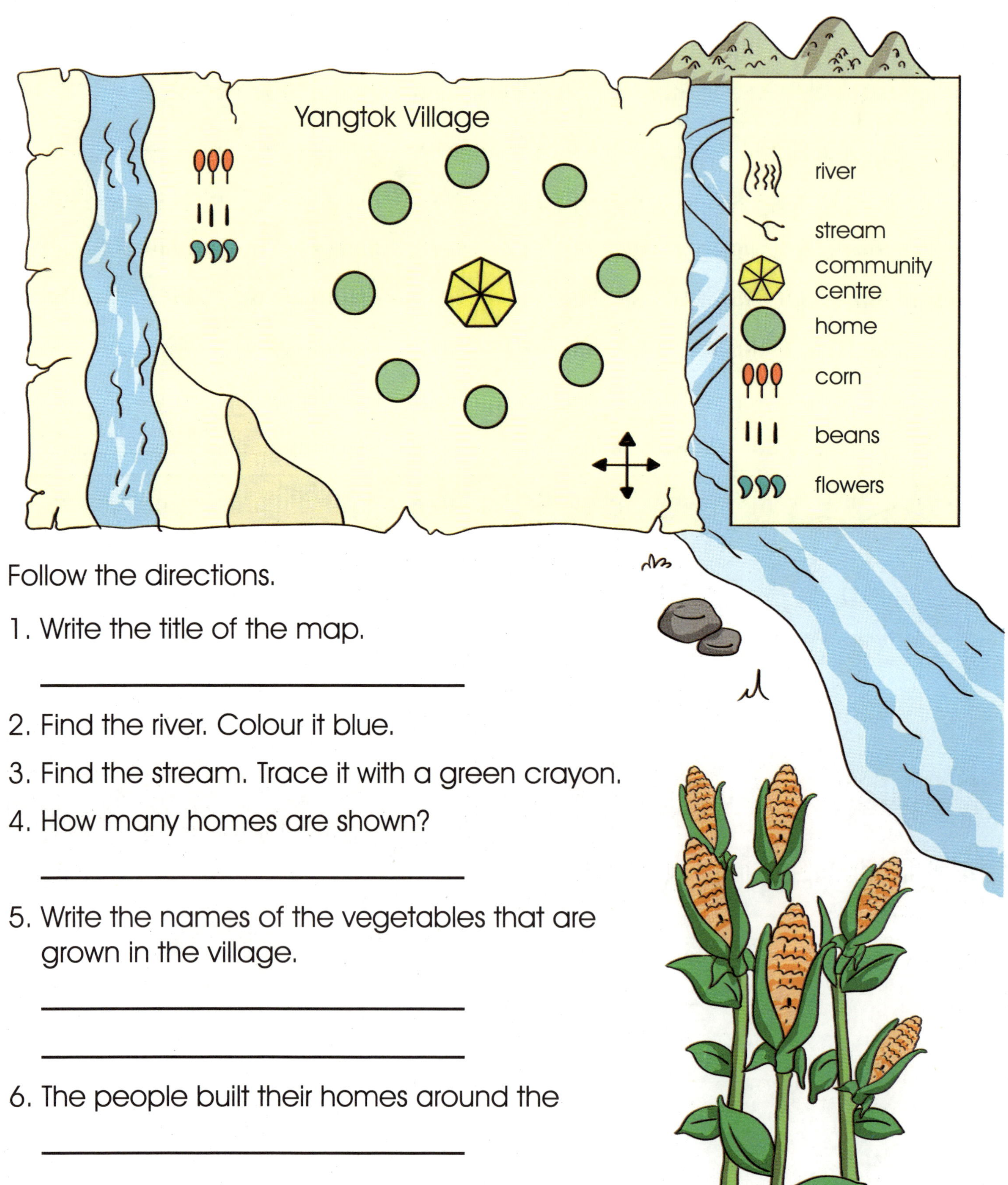

Follow the directions.

1. Write the title of the map.

____

2. Find the river. Colour it blue.
3. Find the stream. Trace it with a green crayon.
4. How many homes are shown?

____

5. Write the names of the vegetables that are grown in the village.

____

____

6. The people built their homes around the

____

Map Skills

Use the map and the key to answer each question.

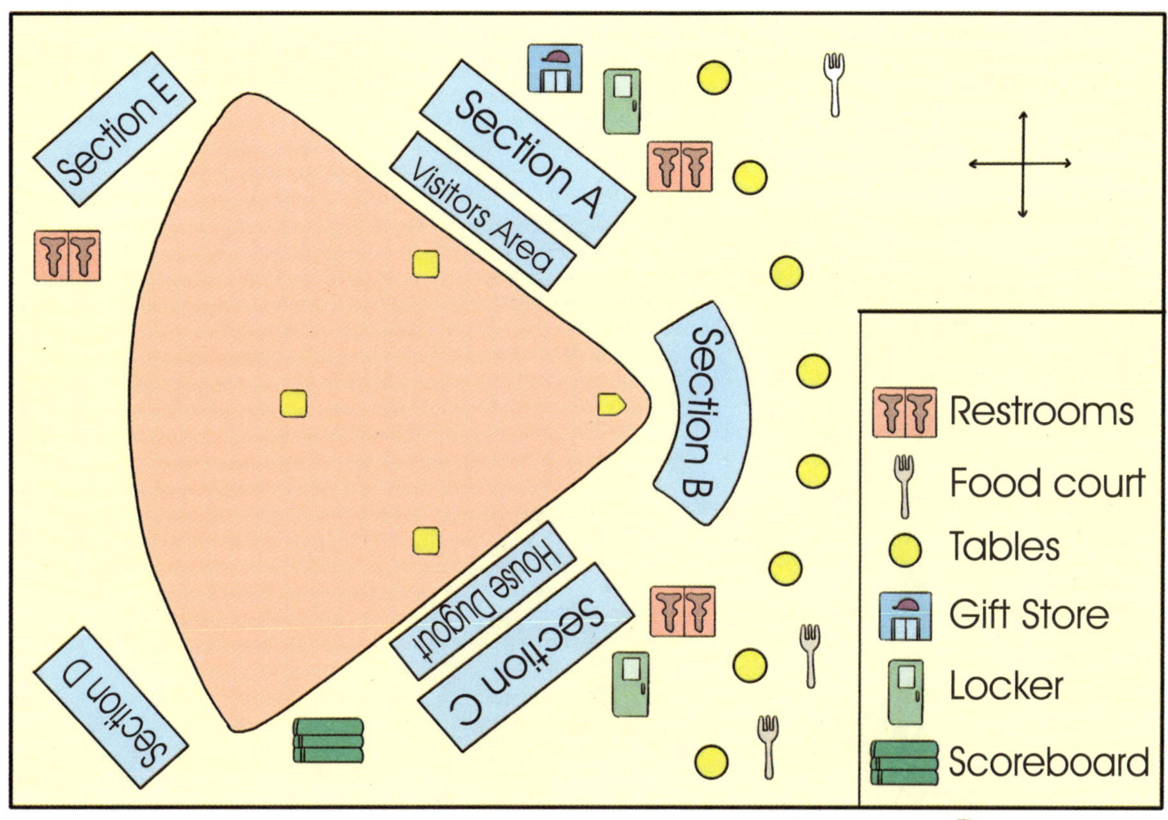

1. How many food courts are there in the picture?
2. Put a tick on the gift store.
3. How many tables are shown in the picture?
4. Draw a circle around the locker room.
5. How many restrooms can you see in the map?
6. Which section is behind the Visitors Area?
7. Where is the scoreboard?
8. Which section is closest to the locker room?

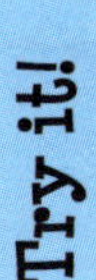

Add one more locker room between Section D and Section E.

Continents

A continent is a large land mass partly or completely separated from other land masses by water. There are 7 continents on Earth.

Look at the map of the world. Unscramble the names of the continents and write them correctly.

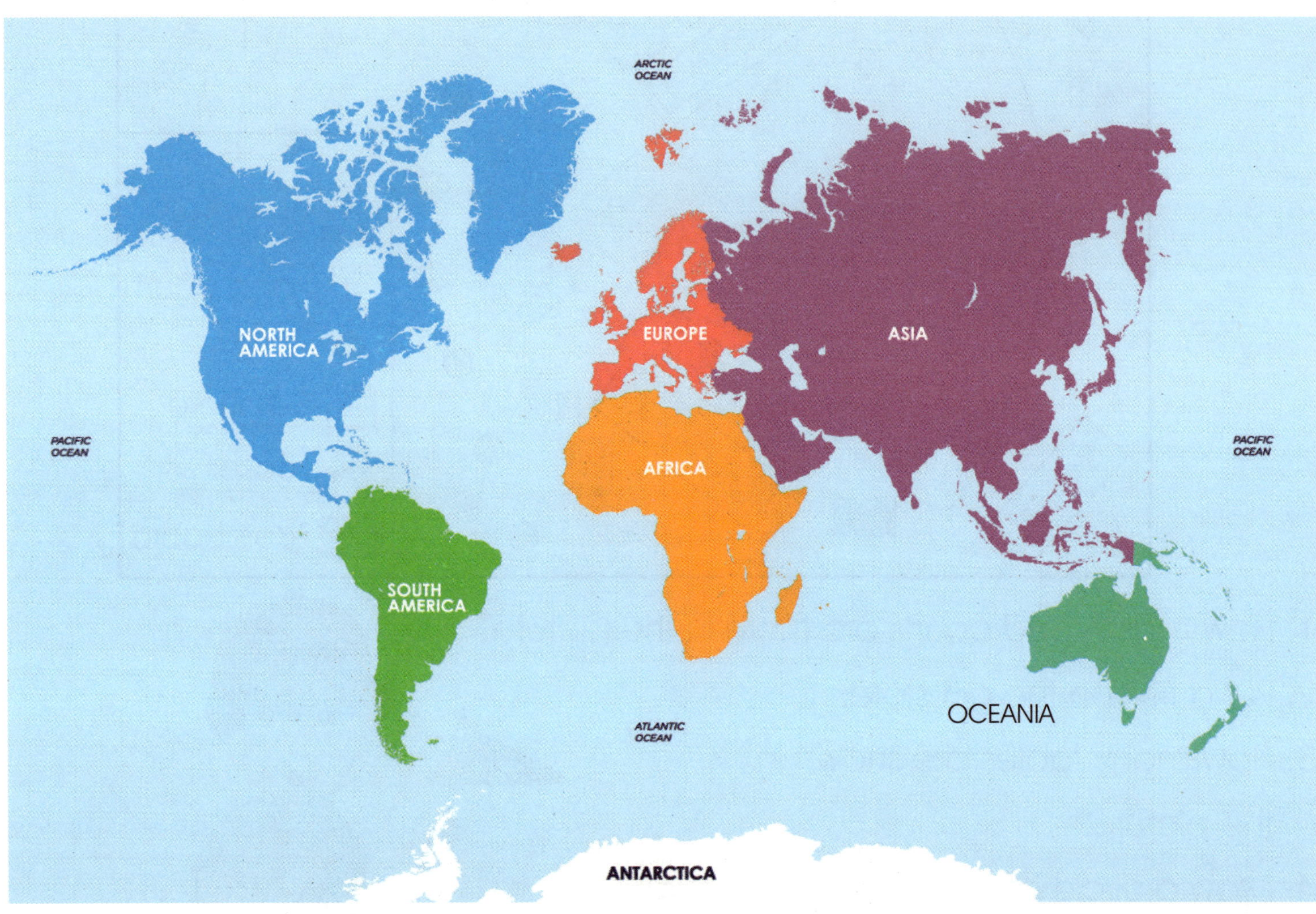

1. SIAA - ______________
2. UROPEE- ______________
3. FRAICA- ______________
4. NTAARCTICA- ______________
5. OUTHS MERAICA- ______________
6. THRON MERAICA- ______________
7. CEANOIA- ______________

Try it!

What was Oceania called earlier? Which countries does it include now?

Oceans

An ocean is a large area of salt water between continents.

There are five oceans in the world.

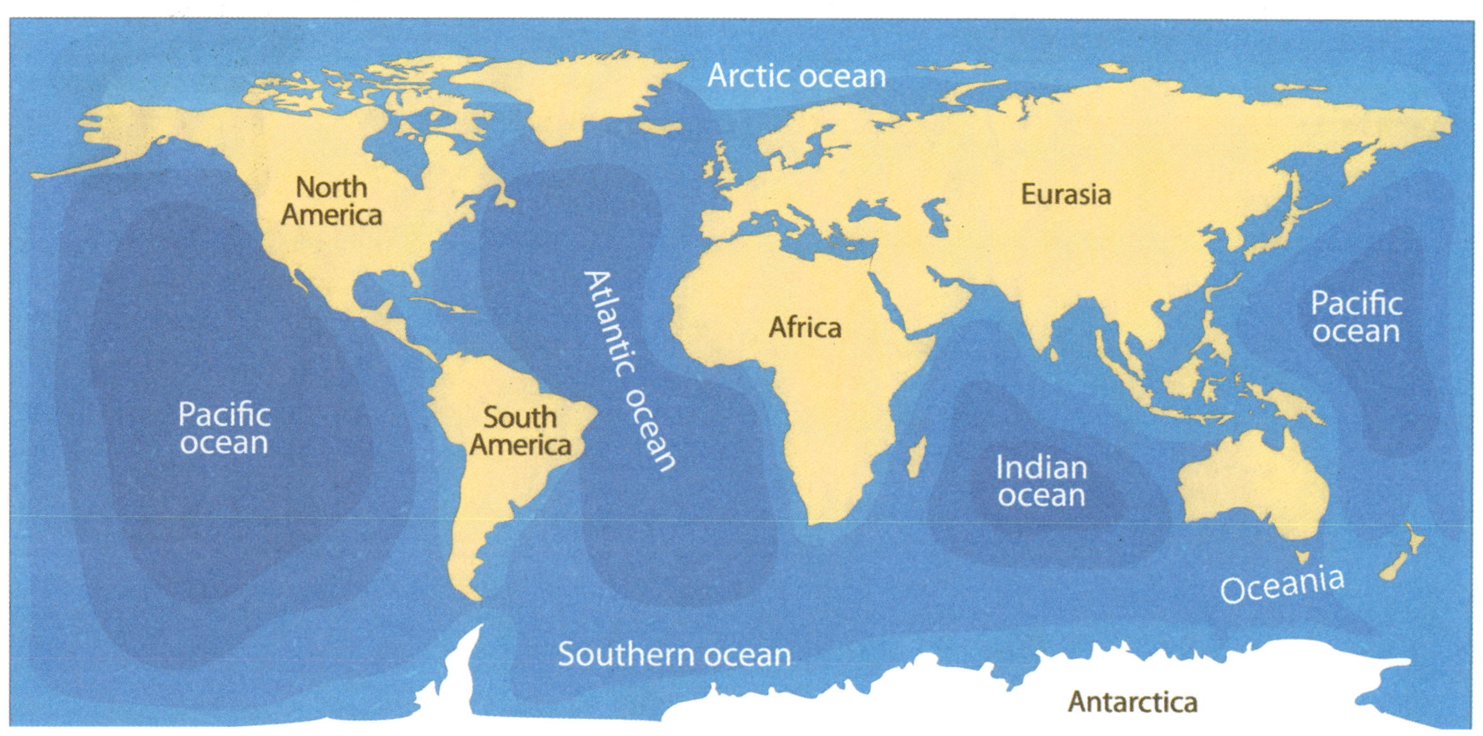

Southern Ocean

Arctic Ocean

Atlantic Ocean

Pacific Ocean

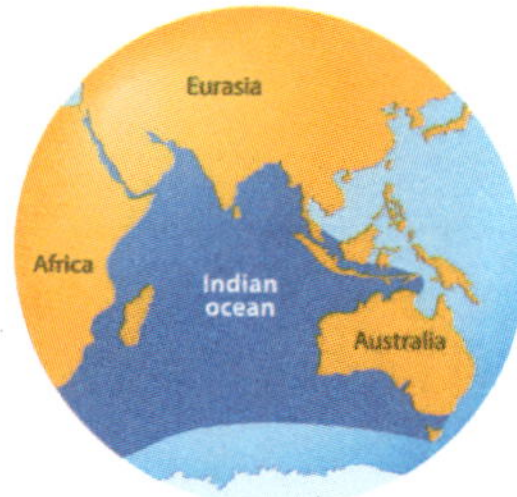

Indian Ocean

Try it!

Find:

Which is the biggest ocean? Where does it lie?

Oceans and Continents

Look at the map and answer the questions.

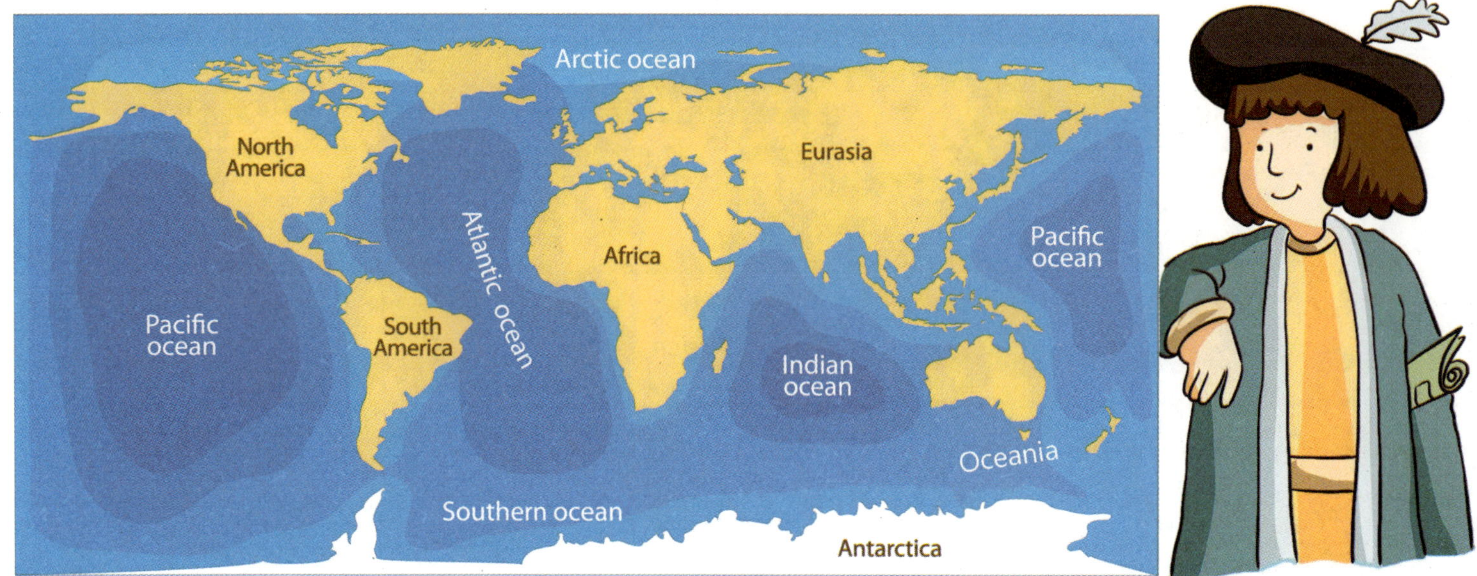

1. How many continents are there in the world?

____

2. Name all the continents.

____

3. Which ocean is to the south of Asia?

____

4. Which ocean can you see between North America and Africa?

____

5. Which continent is to the south of the map?

____

Landforms

Look at the pictures and match the landform to the correct definition.

River

a. A dry piece of land with few animals and plants.

Lake

b. A tall piece of land with steep sides.

Hill

c. A line of water, can be curvy.

Mountain

d. Open land

Desert

e. A small mound

Plain

f. A small body of water with land all around it.

How People Lived Long ago

The things that we do and have, change over time.

Look at the picture.

Talk to your friend about:

a. How has the living of people changed over time?

b. What kind of work people did in the past and where they worked?

c. Were their workplaces far off from their homes?

d. What food do you think they ate?

e. What kind of transportation did people use?

f. Has the equipment people use changed? If so, how?

Now and Then

Look at each object. Circle the ones that were used in the past and are still used now.

Choose any three objects that you did not circle.

Write the name of a different object in each sentence below and complete it.

1. Before there was ______________________________
   people ______________________________
2. Before there was ______________________________
   people ______________________________
3. Before there was ______________________________
   people ______________________________

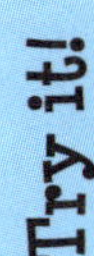

Imagine you lived 2000 years ago. Which modern invention would you miss the most? Why?

Housing Now and Then

Which phrase describes the houses in olden days? Circle Y for yes and N for No.

1. Carpeted floors  

2. Hut made of wood and mud  

3. Kitchen and dishwasher  

4. Mattresses of straw  

5. Straw roofs  

6. Flush in toilets  

7. Air-conditioners  

8. Fireplace as the only heat source  

9. Textured paint  

10. Dirt floors  

11. Electronic doorbell  

12. Benches and stools to sit  

How People Lived Long ago

Speak to your family members or some older persons in your community. Ask them questions on what facilities they had and lacked as a child. How was life different for them?

Then fill in the names and date of birth of the people you interview in the boxes.

Name ______ Date of Birth ______	Name ______ Date of Birth ______	Name ______ Date of Birth ______
Name ______ Date of Birth ______	Name ______ Date of Birth ______	Name ______ Date of Birth ______

Ask your parents about your ancestors. Use the following words in your questions- what, when, why, where and how.

____

____

____

____

____

____

____

Paying for Things

In the past, how did people pay for the things they wanted?

Fill in the blanks by using the words from the box.

Long, long ago, people did not use c__________________ and notes to p__________________ for things. In those days, they used b__________________ system as a way of exchanging goods. If someone had a lot of t__________________ , but not enough food to e__________________ , she or he needed to find someone who would exchange some food for tea. Things such as b__________________, salt, g__________________ , cattle and tea were exchanged. Later people began using pieces of g__________________ and s__________________ to pay for goods. Later, the pieces of metal were used to make c__________________ . Today, we use n__________________ and c________ or bank cards to pay for goods.

pay	tea	eat	silver	beads
coins	gold	barter	grains	notes

Goods and Services Now

Goods are items you buy, such as food, clothing, books, fruits, and toothpaste. A service is an action that a person does for someone else.

Read the text in the box below. Write it under the correct column.

1. Buy vegetables from the Hula Market.
2. Get your car repaired.
3. Go to a music store and buy a CD.
4. Go to the dentist because of a toothache
5. Shop at the bakery and get pastries.
6. Book a painter to paint your house.
7. Shop for woollen clothes and get a cardigan.

Natural Resources

Read each task and think about the resource you need to make it possible. Then use the codes to colour the circles. Write how these resources are useful to us.

○ Breathe	○ Wash hands	○ Blow-up balloons
○ Use coins	○ Swim	○ Plant seeds
○ Use jewellery	○ Eat vegetables	○ Wear cotton clothing

Resource Code

Air- yellow

Water- blue

Soil- brown

Plants- green

Minerals - orange

Try it!

Make a list of 10 natural resources that we use. Then write ways to conserve each natural resource.

Conserving Resources

Saving Earth's resources is called conservation.
Read each conservation tip below and write it in the correct box.

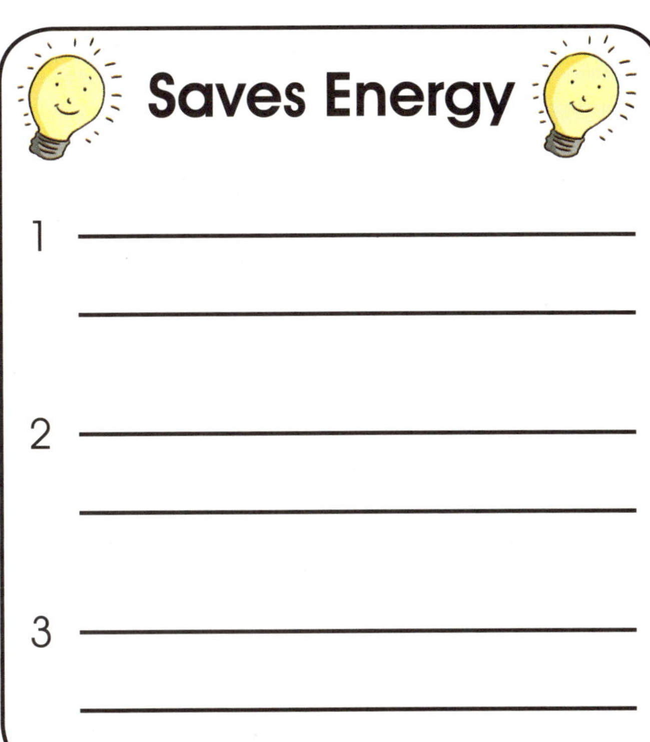

Saves Water

1 ______________________

____

2 ______________________

____

3 ______________________

____

Saves Energy

1 ______________________

____

2 ______________________

____

3 ______________________

____

Saves Paper

1 ______________________

____

2 ______________________

____

3 ______________________

____

Conservation tips

1. Ride a bicycle instead of using a car.
2. Reuse paper.
3. Take showers instead of baths.
4. Close the refrigerator door right away.
5. Turn off taps while brushing your teeth.
6. Recycle newspaper.
7. Turn off electrical appliances when not in use.
8. Write on both sides of paper.
9. Repair leaky faucets.

Answer Key

Page 2

Urban

taxis

subways

museum

skyscrapers

Suburban

house

pool

garden

backyard,

Farm

corn

rural

tractor

horses

Page 3

Children will do on their own. Answers may vary.

Page 4

1. The policemen, firemen and ambulance attendants are helping hands in the picture.
2. The police officer helps the fire fighters in controlling the crowd.
3. Emergency medical services are necessary so that people can be saved and protected in case of mis-happenings.
4. Children will do on their own. Answers may vary.

Page 5

Children will do on their own. Answers may vary.

Page 6

1. your pets
2. Don't run
3. Don't
4. chores
5. homework
6. with your brothers and sisters
7. bike helmet
8. Listen
9. traffic rules
10. Respect

Page 7

My community rights	My community responsibilities
I play at a neighbourhood park.	I reuse as many things as I can.
The people of my community care for each other.	I follow road signs.
I can count on others if I need help.	I help others in need.
I check out books from the library.	I keep my pets from roaming in the community.
My community is a safe place.	I put litter in the dustbin.

Page 8

Children will do on their own. Answers may vary.

Page 9

Children will do on their own. Answers may vary.

Page 10

All the four directions need to be complete in the boxes. The children should write- North, South, East and West

Page 11

1. Southeast
2. West
3. Northeast
4. Northwest
5. South
6. North
7. East
8. Southwest

Page 13

1. From flower display to insect display:
   Move 2 steps east and then move 4 steps north.
2. From help desk to snacks counter:
   Move 3 steps north.
3. From fish display to wildlife display:
   Move 3 steps north.
4. From tree display to maps
   Move 3 steps west and 2 steps north.

Page 14

Children will do on their own.

Page 15

Children will do on their own.

Page 16

1. The title of the map is Yangtok Village.
2. Children will colour the river on their own.
3. Children will circle the stream on their own.
4. The vegetables that grow here are corn and beans.
5. The people have built their homes around the community centre.

Answer Key

Page 17

1. There are three food courts.
2. Children will do on their own.
3. There are eight tables.
4. Children will do on their own.
5. There are three rest rooms.
6. Section A is behind the Visitor's Area.
7. The scoreboard is between section C and section D.
8. Section A is closest to the locker room.

Page 18

1. ASIA
2. EUROPE
3. AFRICA
4. ANTARCTICA
5. SOUTH AMERICA
6. NORTH AMERICA
7. OCEANIA

Page 20

1. There are seven continents in the world.
2. Asia, Europe, Africa, Antarctica, South America, North America, Oceania
3. Indian Ocean
4. Atlantic Ocean
5. Antarctica

Page 21

a. A dry piece of land with few animals and plants- desert
b. A tall piece of land with steep sides- mountain
c. A line of water, can be curvy – river
d. Open land- plain
e. A small mound- hill
f. A small body of water with land all around it- lake

Page 22

Children will do on their own.

Page 23

Children will do on their own.

Page 24

1. Carpeted floors- N
2. Hut made of wood and mud- Y
3. Kitchen and dishwasher- N
4. Mattresses of straw- Y
5. Straw roofs- Y
6. Flush in toilets- N
7. Air-conditioners- no
8. Fireplace as the only heat source- Y
9. Textured paint- N
10. Dirt floors- Y
11. Electronic door bell- N
12. Benches and stools to sit- N

Page 25

Children will do on their own.

Page 26

Coins

pay

barter

tea

eat

beads

grains

gold

silver

coins

notes

coins

Page 27

Children will do on their own.

Page 28

Children will do on their own.

Page 29

Saves water

1. Repair leaky faucets.
2. Turn off taps while brushing your teeth.
3. Take showers instead of baths.

Saves paper

1. Reuse paper.
2. Write on both sides of paper.
3. Recycle newspaper.

Save energy

1. Ride a bicycle instead of using a car.
2. Turn off electrical appliances when not in use.
3. Close the refrigerator door right away.